Contents

Start here

*If you can, ask a teacher or other English speaker for help with reading this.

Who? What? When? How?

Welcome to *Life on Earth and other pieces*, a self-access reader for beginner students of English who have studied approximately the first twelve units of *The New Cambridge English Course* Level 1, or who are at a similar stage of another beginners' course.

With this book, what and when you read is for *you* to decide, and there are many different topics, taken from books, magazines and newspapers to choose from. Most texts have been adapted to make them easier to understand. The texts at the beginning are generally the easier ones, but you can decide where you want to start.

You'll find there are quite a lot of new words in many texts, but try to understand the general meaning first – don't worry about every new word. In fact your reading will improve and your enjoyment will increase if you can learn to understand the general idea quickly before you concentrate on details.

There are tasks with many of the texts. These are marked * and they are there, if you want them, to give you help with difficulties. None of these tasks are tests of memory, so of course you can look at the text while you're doing them. But reading is the most important thing, so if you prefer not to do the task – that's fine.

And also ...

Here are some extra things you can do to help your reading skills in English. You will find more of these in the other three books in *The New Cambridge English Course Readers* series.

- Look at the title at the beginning of a new text. Does it give you an idea of what the text is about? Look quickly at the rest of the text. Were you right?
- Find a text with pictures. How quickly can you find the things in the pictures in the text?
- Choose some new words (not more than about five) to learn from one of the texts.
- Find a text that looks difficult. Read it through without stopping to get an idea of how much you *can* understand.
- Think of a piece of information you found in this book. Try to find it again as quickly as possible.
- Persuade another person to read a text that you like.

What do you do to really relax?

'Take the dog for a walk.'
Nigel, 36, leisure and tourism consultant

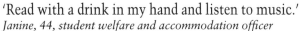

1

'Curl up in bed under a duvet and read.'
Bridget, 16, sixth-form student

'Juggle.'
Emma, 14, secondary-school student

'Lie down.'
Christopher, 10, schoolboy

2

'Lie on the floor and listen to classical music.'
Sue, 42, writer

'Read with a drink in my hand and listen to music.'
Janine, 44, student welfare and accommodation officer

'Draw pictures.'
Jane, 26, craftsperson

'Go fishing.'
Andrew, 30, journalist

'Lie in bed; listen to music with food.'
Sara, 17, student

3

'Read.'
Joan, 62, housewife and grandmother

'Do the gardening.'
Martin, 66, retired architect

'Sit and listen to music.'
Andrew, 36, scientist

'Be with a friend, read a book.'
Monica, 25, student

4

'Sit and watch TV with a cigarette and my knitting.'
Sheila, 37, librarian

'Lie on my bed listening to my stereo.'
Mark, 46, teacher

'Long walks alone or accompanied; read a lot
of books.'
A monk, 66, priest and teacher

5

'Have a long, hot bath.'
Jenny, 29, hairdresser

'Yoga.'
Lynda, 42, translator

'Juggle, lie on the floor or go to bed.'
Pete, 41, engineer

6

'A pint of beer and a game of darts.'
Norman, 54, taxi-driver

'Have a bath with a lot of bubbles.'
Annick, 20, student

7

'I don't relax, that's the problem, so I just think about it.'
Clare, 27, cleaner

'Sit on my bed in my underpants with a beer
and a cigarette, watching television.'
John, 26, driver

'Chat to a friend.'
Yoshimi, 23, student

'Play tennis and golf and bridge.'
James, 43, dentist

8

'Find a place without people.'
Xuemei, 19, student

* Who are the people in the pictures? Match the correct name to
each picture.

Glider

What could be simpler – a Glider with only *two* folds! Be careful to follow the instructions carefully, because it is important to hold and release it in the correct way. Use a 15cm square of thin paper such as origami paper or airmail paper. Heavier paper will not float the design through the air.

1 Fold in half along a diagonal.

2 Fold up the lower edge a little way. Try to keep the crease exactly parallel to the edge.

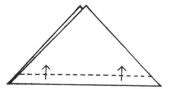

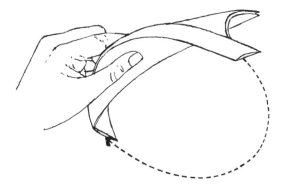

3 Tuck one end of the hem into the pocket at the other end, bending the paper into a circle with the hem on the outside.

4 The Glider is complete. Make sure that the leading edge is a neat circle.

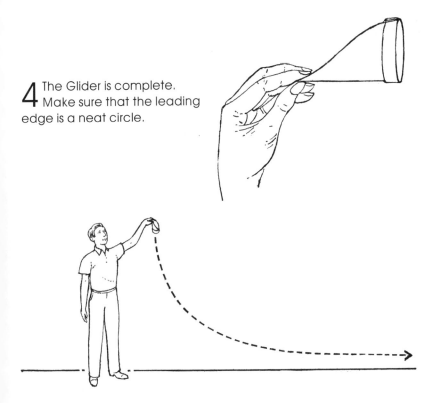

5 Hold as shown, high above your head, with the Glider pointing downwards. Release it gently. It will fall quickly at first, then level out and glide a considerable distance. Remember to release it gently. Never throw or push it.

(from *Classic Origami* by Paul Jackson)

Decibels

The decibel (dB) is the unit used to measure sound. But it is not a constant unit, like a metre or a kilogram. If you increase a sound by 10dB, you make it ten times as loud. So a sound of 20dB is not twice as loud as a sound of 10 dB – it is ten times as loud.
The table here gives an idea of the decibel levels of common sounds that many of us hear in our everyday lives.

Decibel levels of sounds

Intensity	Equivalent decibels	Typical sounds
1	0	The smallest sound the human ear can hear.
10	10	Leaves rustling in the wind.
100	20	Quiet country lane.
1 000	30	A watch ticking. Rustle of paper. Whisper.
10 000	40	Quiet office. Quiet conversation.
100 000	50	Quiet street. Inside average home.
1 000 000	60	Normal conversation at 1m.
10 000 000	70	Busy street. Large shop. Building noise.
100 000 000	80	Danger level. Inside small car. Noisy office. Alarm clock.
1 000 000 000	90	Heavy lorry. Underground train.
10 000 000 000	100	Food blender at 0.6m. Inside train compartment when door is slammed.
100 000 000 000	110	Car horn at 6m. Pop group at 1.3m. Train whistle at 15m.
1 000 000 000 000	120	Sound causes pain. 1 million million times greater than the smallest sound. Jet plane at 150m. Inside factory where boilers are made.
10 000 000 000 000	130	Jet engine at 30m.
100 000 000 000 000	140	
1 000 000 000 000 000	150	Sound can burn skin.
10 000 000 000 000 000	160	
100 000 000 000 000 000	170	
1 000 000 000 000 000 000	180	Sound kills animals and people.
10 000 000 000 000 000 000	190	
100 000 000 000 000 000 000	200	Noise weapon.

(from *Vital Statistics* by Gyles Brandreth)

* Put the decibel numbers with the correct pictures.

200   120   100   100   70   30   20

Summer pudding

* Check the names of the fruits in a dictionary.

This very English pudding is easy to make – and always very popular.

   30ml water
   150g sugar
   450g mixed blackcurrants and blackberries, washed
   100–175g white bread, cut in thin slices
   cream

Stir the water and sugar together and bring slowly to the boil; add the fruits and stew gently, until they are soft but retain their shape.

Cut the crusts from the bread and line a 900ml pudding basin with the slices.

Pour in the fruit and cover with more slices of bread. Place a saucer with a weight on it on top of the pudding and leave overnight in a cool place.

Turn out and serve with cream. Other soft fruits (or a mixture) may be used in summer pudding, providing they have a rich, strong colour – for example, raspberries, redcurrants, plums. A proportion of apple can be included.

(from the *Good Housekeeping Cookery Book*)

Two poems

* Read these poems with a dictionary.

Poem Without an End

Inside the brand-new museum
there's an old synagogue.
Inside the synagogue
is me.
Inside me
my heart.
Inside my heart
a museum.
Inside the museum
a synagogue,
inside it
me
inside me
my heart,
inside my heart
a museum.

Yehuda Amichai, Israel

14

Her greatest love

At sixty she's experiencing
the greatest love of her life.

She walks arm in arm with her lover,
the wind ruffles their grey hair.

Her lover says:
– 'You have hair like pearls.'

Her children say:
– 'You silly old fool.'

Anna 'Swir', Poland

Where did they appear first?

Each of these discoveries or inventions first appeared in a different country. Can you match them?

a) X-ray   Spain

b) ballpoint pen   Denmark

c) sign language   Italy

d) dynamite   USA

e) electric cell   Germany

f) personal stereo   England

g) pneumatic tyre   Japan

h) photocopier   Sweden

i) penicillin   Argentina

j) Lego   Ireland

Answers

a) X-rays were discovered in Germany in 1895 by Wilhelm Röntgen. He was awarded the Nobel Prize for his discovery in 1901.

b) The ballpoint pen was the invention of a Hungarian artist and journalist called Laszlo Biro. He invented the pen in the 1930s, but it was not produced until 1940 in Buenos Aires, Argentina, where Biro had gone to escape from the Second World War. Like many inventors, Biro did not make much money from his discovery.

c) Spain was the country where the first sign language alphabet was developed – as long ago as 1620. It was invented by J. P. Bonnet, a tutor at the Spanish court.

d) Alfred Nobel invented dynamite in Sweden in 1867. The money he made from it was left to the foundation which now awards the Nobel Prizes in Physics, Medicine, Chemistry, Literature and Peace.

e) The electric cell first appeared in Italy in 1800. It was developed by Alessandro Volta, a professor of physics; his name survives as the electrical measure volt.

f) Akio Morita, president of the Japanese company Sony, developed the first personal stereo – the Sony Walkman. Morita, who likes both golf and music, invented the machine so that he could enjoy both hobbies at the same time.

g) John Boyd Dunlop, a Scotsman, thought of making tyres filled with air for his son's bicycle while he was working in Belfast, Ireland. He produced the first tyres in 1888, and by 1894 they were being made for motorcycles as well. They were first used on cars, however, by the Michelin brothers in France.

h) Surprisingly, the first photocopier was invented in 1903 in the USA by an office worker named G. C. Beidler. It was almost 60 years, however, before the machine became widely used.

i) In 1928 Alexander Fleming discovered penicillin while doing medical research in London. The discovery brought him the Nobel Prize for Medicine in 1945.

j) Denmark is the home of Lego. Ole Kirk Christiansen designed Lego bricks in 1955, making up the name from the Danish words *leg godt*, 'to play well'.

Six eyes look at the world

* Read with a dictionary.

Bill Watterson

Bill Watterson is a cartoonist from the USA. One of his creations is a six-year-old boy called Calvin, who spends a lot of time imagining things. Often in the cartoons we see the world first as Calvin sees it, then through the eyes of his parents.

Posy Simmonds

Posy Simmonds is a British cartoonist. One of her favourite subjects is the English middle class – especially their home and family life.

Quino

Quino is a Spanish cartoonist. In his work Quino often attacks bureaucracy; another favourite topic of his is the world of art, music and literature.

I congratulate you, you've got the magic of Chagall!...

... the poetry of Renoir!... ... the vigour of Van Gogh!...   the freedom of Picasso!...   ... the fine touch of Modigliani!

I wanted to be me!

The Peters' projection: a new view of the world

How many times do you think Europe would fit into Africa? Three, maybe? How many times would Spain fit into India? Five or six times?

The answer to these questions depends on your map. The maps above show India six times as big as Spain. But a different kind of map, using the Peters' projection, shows India about eight times as big as Spain. Maps using the Peters' projection show that Africa is more like four times as big as Europe – not three.

The maps we usually use are not in fact correct. After 1492, when Columbus went to the Americas, Europe started to control more and more of the world. The Europeans who made maps showed European countries bigger than they really are. Today many of our maps still show Europe too big. There is another reason why our maps are often not 100% correct: it's impossible to show the round world on a flat piece of paper. But it is possible to correct the European view of the world. This is what Arno Peters did in 1973 when he published his world map.

Think of the countries of the world. How big are they? Then turn the page.

The cities marked on the map are mentioned later in this book, on page 26 and page 27.

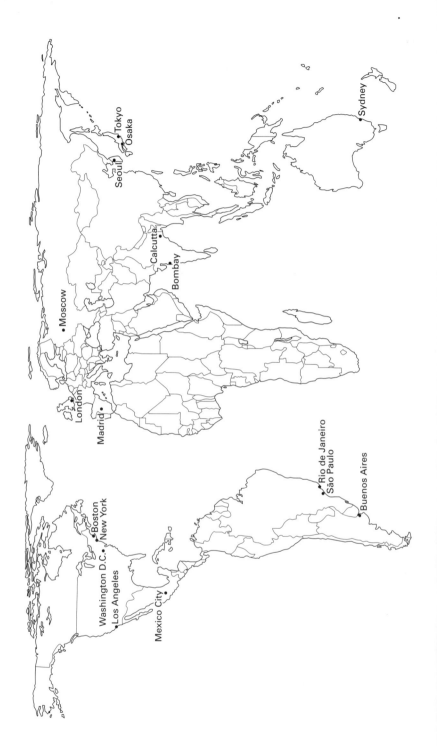

Life on earth

* Read with a dictionary. Look up only the <u>underlined</u> words.

After 3,500 million years of evolution, it is estimated that there are now 3×10^{33}, or 3,000 quintillion (or 3,000,000,000,000,000,000, 000,000,000,000,000) living things on earth.

Of these, 75 per cent are <u>bacteria</u>, and 0.000,000,000,000,000,000, 00013% are human beings.

The <u>Species</u>

There are probably between 5 and 10 million different species of plants, animals and other life-forms on earth. Only a small percentage of these are known, but they include 1,300,000 species of animals and 300,000 species of plants.

There are about three million species of insects, but only one million have names.

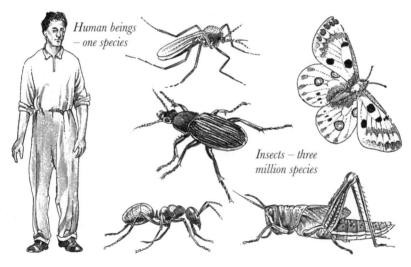

Human beings – one species

Insects – three million species

The Most Successful Species

The most successful form of animal life are insects. They began evolving 1,000 million years before humans, they can live in places where we can't – and there are twelve million of them for every human.

A column of air 1.6 kilometres square, beginning 15 metres above the ground and extending up to 4,270 metres, contains an average of 25 million insects – as well as large quantities of seeds, bacteria and pollen. Most of these are light-bodied insects such as small flies, wasps and lice; but wingless insects, mites and spiders have been found at high altitude.

The most successful life-form of any kind are bacteria. They can withstand 6.5 million roentgens of radiation (650 roentgens will kill a human); they can live in boiling acids, and at the bottom of the sea and, as NASA reported in 1967, they have been found on the edge of space, at a height of 41,150 metres.

The Largest Animal

The smallest animal is a single cell. The largest living animal (and probably the largest there has ever been) is the blue whale. The record is presently held by a female blue whale measuring 34.6 metres. Blue whales (along with rorqual whales and some other species) average out at approximately 4.8 tonnes per metre in length, so this creature weighs more than 170 tonnes. This is the same as 35 elephants, or 2,380 human beings, or 136 million pygmy shrews (the smallest living mammals).

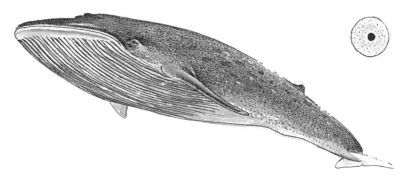

The Fastest Animal

The fastest physical action of any organism is the wing-beat of a common midge (*Forcipomyia*). It normally beats its <u>wings</u> 57,000 times a minute, but it can beat its wings 133,000 times a minute.

The fastest movement in human beings is the blink of an eye, which takes about $1/_{25}$th of a second.

The Human Biomass

At the moment, there are about 5.5 thousand million people on earth. They occupy a volume of 283,000 million cubic metres, and <u>weigh</u> about 115 million tonnes, with an increase of one million tonnes each year.

This is nothing. The insects still outweigh us by three to one.

(from *Animal Oddities* by John May and Michael Marten)

The world's twelve largest cities

Between 1988 and 1990 an American organisation called
Population Crisis Committee did a survey of the world's 100 largest
cities. Among other things they discovered that, of the 100, Lagos is
the worst city to live in, and that Tokyo and Osaka are the best.
Here are some of the things they discovered about the twelve largest
cities. (You can find these twelve cities marked on the map on page 22.)

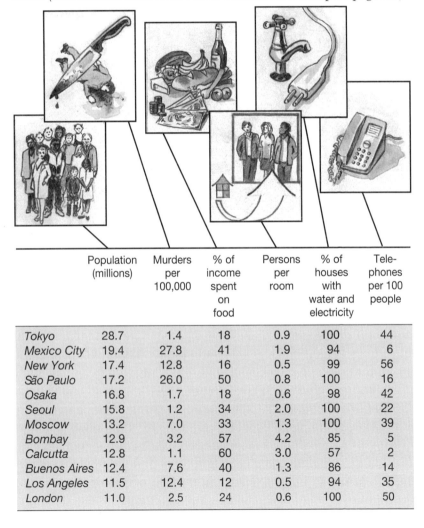

	Population (millions)	Murders per 100,000	% of income spent on food	Persons per room	% of houses with water and electricity	Tele-phones per 100 people
Tokyo	28.7	1.4	18	0.9	100	44
Mexico City	19.4	27.8	41	1.9	94	6
New York	17.4	12.8	16	0.5	99	56
São Paulo	17.2	26.0	50	0.8	100	16
Osaka	16.8	1.7	18	0.6	98	42
Seoul	15.8	1.2	34	2.0	100	22
Moscow	13.2	7.0	33	1.3	100	39
Bombay	12.9	3.2	57	4.2	85	5
Calcutta	12.8	1.1	60	3.0	57	2
Buenos Aires	12.4	7.6	40	1.3	86	14
Los Angeles	11.5	12.4	12	0.5	94	35
London	11.0	2.5	24	0.6	100	50

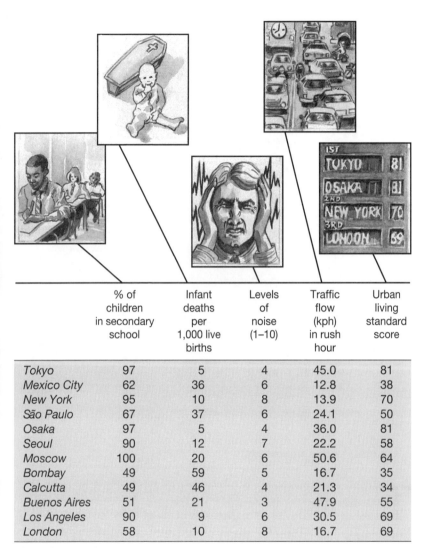

	% of children in secondary school	Infant deaths per 1,000 live births	Levels of noise (1–10)	Traffic flow (kph) in rush hour	Urban living standard score
Tokyo	97	5	4	45.0	81
Mexico City	62	36	6	12.8	38
New York	95	10	8	13.9	70
São Paulo	67	37	6	24.1	50
Osaka	97	5	4	36.0	81
Seoul	90	12	7	22.2	58
Moscow	100	20	6	50.6	64
Bombay	49	59	5	16.7	35
Calcutta	49	46	4	21.3	34
Buenos Aires	51	21	3	47.9	55
Los Angeles	90	9	6	30.5	69
London	58	10	8	16.7	69

(from the *Guardian*)

Population Crisis Committee also found that, of the 100 cities, Cape Town is the most violent – 65 murders per 100,000 people. Lima is the slowest; traffic flow in the rush hour is only 6kph. And the three cities with 100% of 14–17-year-olds at school? They are Moscow, Warsaw and Essen.

The earth at night

EARTH at NIGHT

* Read this with a dictionary.

This is the earth at night – the first picture created to show the patterns of light and darkness on our planet. It was made from photographs taken between 1974 and 1984 by satellites belonging to the US Air Force. These satellites take hundreds of photos every day, recording information about the world's weather. Woodruff T. Sullivan III, an American professor of astronomy, looked at thousands of these photos to find the clearest ones. Finally he chose about 40 photos which were put together to make the picture you see here.

What we see when we look at the earth at night are the lights of cities and roads, and also fires. Madrid is clearly visible in the middle of the picture, and it is quite easy to find Rio de Janeiro, Moscow, London and Sydney. The bright area on the east coast of the USA is Washington, New York and Boston*. The fires we can see are mostly gas burning in oil-fields. Two big ones are at Sulawesi, Indonesia (north of western Australia) and in Siberia (the large bright area in the top

*You can find all these cities marked on the map on page 22.

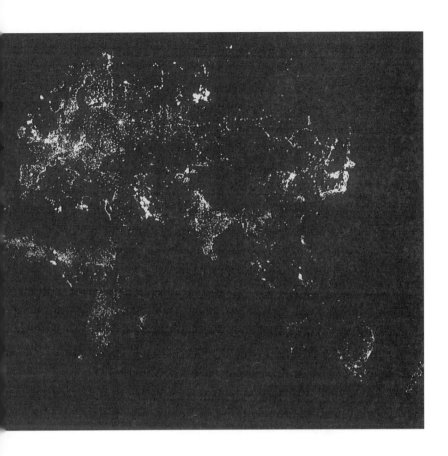

right of the picture), while the biggest of all shows us clearly the oilfields of Saudi Arabia and the Gulf states. In east Africa we can see grassland burning, where poor populations try to get more grass for their animals by burning grazing land.

Not all the bright areas are fires or the lights of cities and roads, however. To the west of Japan in the Sea of Japan there is a huge fleet of fishing boats. The boats are using lights to bring squid to the surface of the sea.

What we *can't* see is in some ways as interesting as what we can see. The burning of tropical forests, as for instance in the Amazon, doesn't show up too well on the image here – there's too much smoke. Also compare the brightness of the USA, western Europe, and Japan with the darkness of Asia, Africa and South America (25% of the world's population use about 75% of the world's electricity). Why, also, are Britain and Belgium much brighter than France or the east of Germany? And, finally, why do the rich nations waste so much energy while the poor ones are burning their environment?

How you use water (if you live in the United States)

Which uses more water – washing your clothes, or taking a bath? Does it take more water to produce a kilogram of flour or a litre of whisky? How much water is needed to make a new car – 3,785 litres, 37,850 litres or 378,500 litres? Keep reading to find the right answers.

Direct personal use – 8% of the nation's total, or 605 litres per person per day, is used for personal and home activities:

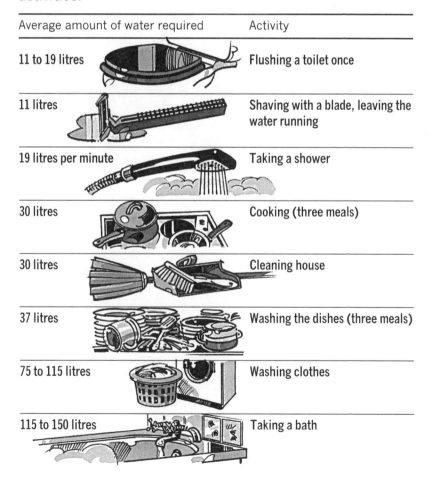

Average amount of water required	Activity
11 to 19 litres	Flushing a toilet once
11 litres	Shaving with a blade, leaving the water running
19 litres per minute	Taking a shower
30 litres	Cooking (three meals)
30 litres	Cleaning house
37 litres	Washing the dishes (three meals)
75 to 115 litres	Washing clothes
115 to 150 litres	Taking a bath

Agricultural use – about 33% of the nation's total, or 2,270 litres per person per day, is used in farm and ranch operations:

Average amount of water required		Food produced
150 litres		One egg
230 litres		One litre of whisky
300 litres		One ear of corn
567 litres		One loaf of bread
628 litres		One kg of flour
21,020 litres		One kg of beef

Industrial use – about 59% of the nation's total, or 3,930 litres per person per day, is consumed in the production of material goods:

Average amount of water required		Product
6.5 to 25 litres		One litre of petrol
290 litres		One kg of steel
1,060 litres		One Sunday newspaper
2,520 litres		One kg of synthetic rubber
8,410 litres		One kg of aluminium
378,500 litres		One new car

Note: About 2,725 litres per person per day is used for cooling water for electrical power plants.

(from *The Real Cost* by Richard North)

Marriage lines

* Read with a dictionary, choosing not more than five or six words.

Marriage – greatest age difference

The greatest difference in age between marrying adults is 88 years in the case of Imam Ali Azam, 104, and his bride, 16-year-old Marium Begum, from the village of Fateabad, Chittagong, Bangladesh.

Weddings

The record for the most weddings in a lifetime is held by King Mogut of Siam (now Thailand) (the king played by Yul Brynner in the film 'The King and I'). During his reign he had 9,016 wives, all married at different times.

Bigamy

On 31 December 1981, police in Florida, USA, said that Giovanni Vigliotto had married 82 different women since 1949. On 1 February 1983, Vigliotto, then aged 53, told the court in Phoenix, Arizona, that he had in fact married 115 times, including four times in three weeks while on holiday in the Caribbean with a friend in 1968. On 28 March 1983 he was sentenced to 28 years in prison and fined $336,000.

Wedding train

When Karl-Heinz Woike and his bride Andrea Thyssen were married in Hamburg, Germany, more than 600 children from local youth clubs were left outside the church. They were all needed to support Andrea's wedding train. It was nearly 1 kilometre long and it encircled the local shopping centre.

(from *The Third W.H. Allen Alternative Book of Records*)

How well do you know your body?

True or false?

1) Children have more bones than adults.

2) One in ten of the Apollo astronauts was left-handed.

3) In developed countries (the USA and Italy, for example) women live an average of three years longer than men.

4) The hairs on top of your head last longer than the hairs in your eyebrows and eyelashes.

5) In a normal day you blink about 12,000 times.

6) The tallest man who ever lived was 2.72m tall.

7) The first heart transplant took place in December 1971.

8) The heart of a new-born baby beats about twice as fast as the heart of an adult.

9) By the age of two, boys have grown to more than half of their adult height, girls less than half.

10) There is enough carbon in the human body to make 900 pencils.

Which is correct?

11) The smallest bone in the human body is in   a) the nose
                                                    b) the hand
                                                    c) the ear.

12) Your fingernails grow   a) 0.05cm a week
                              b) 0.05cm a fortnight
                              c) 0.05cm a month.

13) The area of skin on the average man's body is   a) $1.85m^2$
                                                                      b) $2.25m^2$
                                                                      c) $2.45m^2$.

14) To stay alive for 24 hours resting in bed, a 64kg man needs
  a) 1,400 calories
  b) 1,550 calories
  c) 1,600 calories.

15) A woman of the same weight needs   a) 1,400 calories
                                                         b) 1,550 calories
                                                        c) 1,600 calories.

16) This scale compares the fastest running speed of some animals.

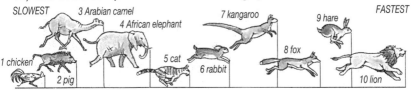

SLOWEST   3 Arabian camel   7 kangaroo   9 hare   FASTEST
4 African elephant   8 fox
1 chicken   5 cat   6 rabbit
2 pig   10 lion

Where would you put a human being in this scale?

17) By the age of 50, how many European men show signs of baldness?
    a) 25%
    b) 33%
    c) 50%.

18) The skin on the soles of your feet is   a) 12 times
                                            b) 15 times
                                            c) 20 times
                                            as thick as the skin on your
                                            eyelids.

19) The water in an average human body would fill   a) 45 litre bottles
                                                          b) 55 litre bottles
                                                           c) 65 litre bottles.

20) The greatest number of children ever born to one mother was   a) 43
                                                                              b) 55
                                                                                c) 69.

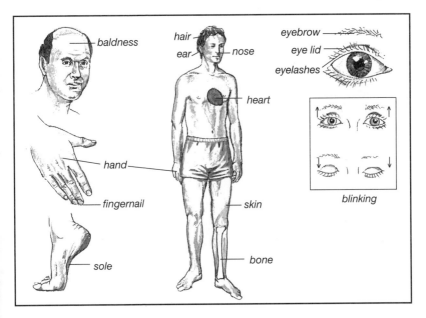

baldness   hair   eyebrow
ear   nose   eye lid
eyelashes
heart
hand
fingernail   skin   blinking
sole   bone

Answers

1) True. Children have between 300 and 350 bones at birth; as they grow, some of the bones join together. An adult has 206 bones.
2) False. One in four was left-handed, compared with one in ten in the population in general.
3) False. Women in these countries live for six to seven years longer than men.
4) True. The hairs in your eyebrows and eyelashes last for three to five months, while the hairs on top of your head can last for up to six years.
5) False. You blink about 17,000 times.
6) True. He was Robert Wadlow (1918–1940), an American.
7) False. It was in December 1967.
8) True. A baby's heart beats about 140 beats a minute; an adult's beats about 70–75 a minute.
9) False. Boys have reached 49.5% of their final height, girls 52.8%
10) True.
11) c) The ear. A bone in the middle ear measures between 2.6 and 3.4mm.
12) a) 0.05cm a week.
13) a) 1.85m². The average woman has 1.57m² on her body.
14) b) 1,550 calories.
15) a) 1,400 calories.
16) A human being is faster than an African elephant but slower than a cat.
17) c) 50%
18) a) 12 times as thick.
19) a) 45 litre bottles.
20) c) 69. The first wife of Feodor Vassilyev, a peasant living near Moscow, had sixteen pairs of twins, seven sets of triplets and four sets of quadruplets between 1725 and 1765.
$(16 \times 2 + 7 \times 3 + 4 \times 4 = 69.)$

A zoo-keeper's day

John Partridge works in Bristol Zoo in the west of England. Here he describes a typical day's work.

There are sixteen kinds of mammal and one kind of bird in my section at the moment. This mixture of different kinds of animals makes this section an interesting one. The animals vary in size from a zebra weighing around 250 kilograms to a prairie dog of about two kilos. The only birds we have are a colony of cockatiels. There are two full-time and two part-time keepers working in this section, making sure that the animals remain fit and healthy.

A typical day starts at eight o'clock. I walk around the section looking for births, deaths or any other problems. Some animals need special care: those that are going to give birth soon, those that were unusually quiet on the previous day, and animals that have just arrived at the zoo.

After this I complete a Daily Report Sheet, which I give to the Head Keeper each day, recording what is happening in my section. Three times a week I also order the food for the animals. Each section has its own small kitchen where we prepare the food.

Next we clean the animal enclosures. In the main building one keeper cleans the five stalls where the zebras sleep at night, and puts down clean straw. At the other end of the building another keeper cleans out the tapirs, muntjac deer and Brazilian agouti rodents.

The enclosures around the main building have to be cleaned too. Other jobs here include watering the plants in the sloth enclosure and changing the peccary's drinking water.

Peccary

Tapir

Muntjac deer

Brazilian
agouti

When we've finished we take all the rubbish to the rubbish skip. Three times a week we collect fresh food for the animals and take it back to our kitchen. The variety of food is good and includes fish for the seals, maize, oats and dairy nuts for the zebras and tapirs, and various types of fruit and vegetables for the monkeys. For some animals we put food in different places around the enclosure, so they have to look for their food, just like animals in the wild.

There is a tea break at ten thirty, and then we spend a couple of hours preparing the food for all the section's animals. In particular we need to make sure that the food is ready for the seals by eleven thirty, because many people come to watch them chasing their fish. After this the keepers have their lunch.

Afternoon work varies but usually includes feeding the animals and tidying up – raking leaves in the autumn, for example, which is a boring job.

Observing the animals and recording data is important too. For example, we are keeping a daily record of the development of the baby seal; this will be useful for us in future, and it may be useful to other zoos too.

At three thirty there is another public feed for the fur seals. We hide vitamin tablets in the fish to keep the seals healthy. Then it's time to bring the zebras in for their tea and clean their enclosure, and then look around the section one last time before going home at five o'clock. Of course, in the summer the Zoo stays open later and staff stay too.

* **Find the names of the animals.**

1 weighs 250kg and eats maize, oats and dairy nuts

2 weighs about 2kg

3 the only birds in the section

4 has plants in its enclosure

5 eats fish (with vitamin tablets)

6 eats fruit and vegetables

Answers

What do you do to really relax?

1 Norman	5 Bridget
2 Sheila	6 Martin
3 Lynda	7 James
4 Andrew	8 Emma

Decibels

1 100 2 20 3 100 4 120
5 70 6 30 7 200

A zoo-keeper's day

1 zebra	4 sloth
2 prairie dog	5 seal
3 cockatiels	6 monkey

Acknowledgements

We would like to thank all the friends and relations who have helped and contributed in various ways, and in particular Bridget, Emma and Lynda Newbery, Andrew Young, Martin Fisher, Sheila Potash, Norman Hewitt and James Carmody. We are also grateful for the constant help and support of colleagues and students at Filton College, Bristol, and for the valuable assistance we have had from the Avon Library Information Service.

Our thanks also to Catherine Boyce, Peter Donovan and Peter Ducker of Cambridge University Press, and to Alison Field of Working with Words, for their indispensable assistance and support.

Lastly we are grateful to Catherine Walter and Michael Swan for their guidance, their suggestions, their time and their encouragement.

The authors and publishers are grateful to the following for permission to reproduce photographs, illustrations and texts. It has not been possible to identify the sources of all the material used, and in such cases the publishers would welcome information from the copyright holders.

Quintet Publishing Ltd for the adapted extract from *Classic Origami* by Paul Jackson, on pp. 8–9; National Magazine Company Ltd for the adapted extract from the *Good Housekeeping Cookery Book*, on pp. 12–13; Universal Press Syndicate for the cartoon by Bill Watterson on p. 18; the Peters Fraser & Dunlop Group Ltd for the cartoon by Posy Simmonds, on p. 19; Editorial Lumen SA for the cartoon by Quino, on p. 20; Peters World Map for the map on p. 22; Abner Stein for the adapted extract by John May and Michael Marten, on pp. 23–5; the *Guardian* for the adapted extract from an article first published on 29/12/90, on pp. 26–7; Hansen Planetarium Publications for the photo, on pp. 28–9; Richard North for the adapted extract from *The Real Cost* 1986, on pp. 30–1; Virgin Publishing Ltd for the adapted extract from the *WH Allen Alternative Book of Records* by Mike Barwell, on pp. 32–3, Bristol, Clifton & West of England Zoological Society for the adapted extract from *Noah's Bark* Vol. 1 Issue 3, on pp. 37–9.

Drawings by Peter Byatt, Celia Chester, David Cook, Harriet Dell, David Downton, Helena Greene, Tony Hall, Leslie Marshall, Edward McLachlan and Kaoru Miyake.

Book designed by Peter Ducker MSTD